About the Author

Mrs. Susan Thomas has 10 years of experience in Excel Formulae and Macros. She has worked on many excel VBA Projects.

Her hobbies are travelling to new tourist places, watching football, cricket and learning latest technological stuff.

Preface

This book covers all Excel functions (2014) and macro. Excel is widely used across world. Knowing excel Formulae is always a step forward in one's skillsets.

Major topics covered in this book are.

1. Introduction to Excel Formulae
2. String Formulae
3. Date and Time Formulae
4. Maths and Trigonometric Formulae
5. Lookup Formulae
6. Logical Formulae
7. Information Formulae
8. Financial Formulae
9. Statistical Formulae
10. Engineering Formulae
11. Database Formulae.
12. User Defined Formulae.
13. VBA Editor
14. VBA Programming Basics
15. Writing and running macros
16. Automating workbook tasks
17. Automating worksheet tasks
18. Automating daily excel tasks
19. Working with pivot table and charts.

1. Excel Introduction

1.1 Overview

Microsoft Excel is one of the product in microsoft office suite of products. It is the most popular spread sheet application used around the world. It is a licensed software from Microsoft.

1.2 Function Categorization

In this book, you will find all microsoft excel Formulae with real life examples. I have categorized the examples as listed below.

1. String Formulae
2. Date and Time Formulae
3. Maths and Trigonometric Formulae
4. Lookup Formulae
5. Logical Formulae
6. Information Formulae
7. Financial Formulae
8. Statistical Formulae
9. Engineering Formulae
10. Database Formulae.
11. User Defined Formulae.

2. String Formulae

2.1 Finding the length of String.

We can find the length of the string using LEN function in Excel.

Example –

=LEN("OBAMA")

Output of above formula will be **5**.

2.2 Finding the Character for ASCII value

We can find the character for numerical value using CHAR function in Excel.

Example –

=CHAR(65)

Output of above formula will be A.

2.3 Removing the Non-Printable characters

We can remove the Non-Printable characters from the cell value using CLEAN function in Excel.

As shown in below image, we CLEAN function is used to remove 2 Dots from B4 cell.

The output is shown in B5 cell.

	A	B
1	Function	Output
2	char(65)	A
3	char(112)	p
4		
5		•text•
6	=CLEAN(B4)	text
7		

2.4 Finding the ASCII value

We can find the ASCII value a character using CODE function in Excel.

Example –

=CODE("A")

Output of above formula will be 65.

2.5 Capitalizing the string

Capitalizes the first letter in a text string and any other letters in text that follow any character other than a letter. Converts all other letters to lowercase letters.

=PROPER("Obama is a President")	Obama Is A President

2.6 Replacing the part of string

We can replace the part of the string using replace function. In below example, we have replaced the 3 characters starting from 2nd position of the OBAMA with Sagar. The ouput is Osagara.

=REPLACE("Obama",2,3,"Sagar")	OSagara

The second parameter is the starting position from where we want to replace the string. The third parameter specifies the number of characters we want to replace.

2.7 Repeat the pattern

We can repeat the pattern using REPT function. The first paramter is the pattern we want to repeat and second paramter is the number of times we want to repeat the pattern.

=REPT("$",3)	$$$
=REPT("AB",3)	ABABAB

2.8 Extracting the part of the string from right side

We can extract the specified number of characters from the right side using RIGHT function. The second parameter specifies how many characters have to be extracted. In first example below, we have extracted 2 characters from right side of the string. In second example, we have not specified the second parameter. So by default it will extract last character from the string.

=RIGHT("OBAMA",2)	MA
=RIGHT("OBAMA")	A

2.9 Searching the string for other string.

We can check whether the string has other string in it using Search function. The first parameter is the string to be searched. Second parameter is the string in which we have to search. The last parameter is the optional parameter which specifies the starting position from where we have to search.

In first example mentioned below, we are searching the BA in OBAMA starting from 2nd position. As BA exists in OBAMA at 2nd position, output is 2. If the string is not found, #VALUE! Is returned.

=SEARCH("BA","OBAMA",2)	2
=SEARCH("BA","OBAMA")	2
=SEARCH("BA","OBNAMA")	#VALUE!

2.10 Substitute the part of string with other string

We can substitutet the part of string with other string using SUBSTITUTE method. We have replaced BA with SA in first example below. While in second example, we have replaced A by K. In second example, we have used third parameter to specify which occurance has to be substituted. As we have passed 2, the 2nd occurance of the A is substituted by K.

=SUBSTITUTE("OBAMA","BA","SA")	OSAMA
=SUBSTITUTE("OBAMA","A","K",2)	OBAMK

2.11 Convert the String to upper case.

We can convert the string to upper case using UPPER function in Excel.

=UPPER("obama")	OBAMA

2.12 Remove the spaces from the String.

We can remove the blank spaces in the string using TRIM function. Please note that trim function will remove the spaces from the beginning and end of the string only. To remove the spaces from the middle of the string, we can use SUBSTITUTE function.

=TRIM("sasas ddsd vc ")	sasas ddsd vc
=SUBSTITUTE("OBA MA"," ","")	OBAMA

2.13 Formatting the String in Excel.

We can format the string using TEXT function. In the second parameter, you have to specify the format of the string.

=TEXT(12343,"$0.00")	$12343.00
=TEXT(12343,"$#,##0.00")	$12,343.00

3. Date and Time Formulae

3.1 Date function

We can use DATE function to create the date from the date parts as mentioned below.

=DATE(1986,1,9)	09-01-1986

3.2 DateValue function

We can use DATEVALUE function to get the numerical representation of the given date.

=DATEVALUE("09-01-1986")	31421

3.3 Getting the day from given date

We can use DAY function to get the day for given date.

=DAY(NOW())	10
=DAY("09-01-1986")	9

3.4 Getting the current timestamp of the system

We can use NOW function to get the current timestamp.

=NOW()	10-05-2014 10:47

3.5 Extracting the Hour part from the given timestamp.

We can use HOUR function to extract the Hour part of the timestamp.

=HOUR(NOW())	10
=HOUR(TIMEVALUE("09-01-1986 11:11:11 AM"))	11

3.6 Extracting the Minute part from the given timestamp.

We can use Minute function to extract the Minute part of the timestamp.

=MINUTE(NOW())	47
=MINUTE(TIMEVALUE("09-01-1986 11:12:13 AM"))	12

3.7 Extracting the Second part from the given timestamp.

We can use Second function to extract the Second part of the timestamp.

=SECOND(NOW())	14
=SECOND(TIMEVALUE("09-01-1986 11:12:13 AM"))	13

3.8 Getting current date of the system.

We can use TODAY function to print the current date.

=TODAY()	10-05-2014

3.9 Getting Weekday for given date.

We can use WEEKDAY function to get the weekday number of the given date.

=WEEKDAY(NOW(),1)	7

For example if the data falls on Sunday, it will return 1, for Monday it will return 2.

3.10 Extracting Year from the given date.

We can use YEAR function to extract the year from the given date.

=YEAR(NOW())	2014
=YEAR("09-01-1986")	1986

3.11 Finding the difference between 2 dates in terms of years.

We can use YEARFRAC function to find the difference between 2 dates.

=YEARFRAC("09-01-1986",NOW(),2)	28.35068493
=YEARFRAC("09-01-2014",NOW(),2)	0.336111111
=YEARFRAC("09-01-2014","09-07-2014",2)	0.502777778

3.12 Finding the future/Past business day.

We can find future or past date using WORKDAY function. Note that WORKDAY function returns the number that must be converted to date using DATE function. This function will exclude the weekends. You can also exclude the holidays using 3rd parameter.

In below example, WORKDAY function returns 41649. Then we have used DATE function to convert this number to date which is nothing but 10-Jan-2014.

=WORKDAY("09-01-2014",1)	41649
=DATE(YEAR(A30), MONTH(A30), DAY(A30))	10-01-2014

In above example, we have added 1 day to 09-Jan-2014. To subtract 1 day we can use below syntax.

=WORKDAY("09-01-2014",-1)	41647
=DATE(YEAR(A30), MONTH(A30), DAY(A30))	08-01-2014

3.13 Finding the number of business days between 2 dates

We can use NETWORKDAYS function to find the number of business days between 2 dates. This function will exclude the weekends. You can also exclude the holidays using 3rd parameter.

=NETWORKDAYS("09-01-1986","09-02-1986")	22

As shown in above example, there are 22 working days between 09-Jan-1986 and 09-Feb-1986. We have not specified holidays list in the third parameter.

3.14 Finding the Month number for given date.

We can use MONTH function to get the numerical representation for the month.

=MONTH(NOW())	5
=MONTH("09-01-1986")	1

3.15 Adding Months to given date.

We can add months to given date using EDATE function. In below example, EDATE function returns 31452. Then we have used DATE function to convert this number to date which is nothing but 09-Feb-1986.

=EDATE("09-01-1986",1)	31452

=DATE(YEAR(B42), MONTH(B42), DAY(B42))	09-02-1986

Here we have added 1 month to the date 09-Jan-1986.

4. Maths and Trigonometrical Formulae

4.1 Finding the absolute value of the number.

We can find the absolute value of the given number using ABS function.

=ABS(12)	12
=ABS(-12)	12

4.2 Find the Ceiling (Largest and Nearest integer) of the number.

We can use CEILING function to find the ceiling of the number.

=CEILING(1.2,1)	2

4.3 COMBIN function

We use COMBIN function to find the number of combinations for a given number of items.

=COMBIN(8,2)	28

4.4 Convert the radians to Degree.

We can use DEGREES function to convert radians to the degrees.

=DEGREES(PI())	180

To convert the degrees to radian, we can use RADIANS function.

=RADIANS(180)	3.141592654

4.5 EVEN and ODD function

We can use EVEN function to find the nearest even number.

=EVEN(4.3)	6
=EVEN(-4.6)	-6

We can use ODD function to find the nearest odd number.

=ODD(3.2)	5

4.6 Finding the e^n

We can use find the e^n using EXP function as shown in below example (e^2).

=EXP(2)	7.389056099

4.7 Finding the factorial of the number.

We can use FACT function to find the factorial of the number.

=FACT(4)	24

4.8 Finding the double factorial of the number.

We can use FACT function to find the factorial of the number.

If number is even, $n!! = n(n-2)(n-4)...(4)(2)$

If number is odd, $n!! = n(n-2)(n-4)...(3)(1)$

=FACTDOUBLE(4)	8

4.9 Finding the floor (Smallest and Nearest integer) of the number.

We can use FLOOR function to find the floor of the given number.

=FLOOR(2.3,1)	2
=FLOOR(-2.3,1)	-3

4.10 Finding the GCD and LCM.

We can use GCD function to find the GCD of 2 or more numbers.

=GCD(4,6)	2

We can find the LCM using LCM function.

=LCM(5,15)	15

4.11 Finding the integer portion of the number.

We can get the integer portion of the number using INT function. Anything after decimal is truncated.

=INT(2.3)	2
=INT(-2.3)	-3

4.12 Logarithmic Formulae in Excel.

Excel provides below Formulae to perform logarithmic operations.

=LN(10)	2.302585093
=LOG(10,10)	1
=LOG10(10)	1

4.13 Find the remainder and Quotient.

We can use MOD function to find the remainder after division. For example – After dividing the 5 by 2, we get the remainder as 1.

=MOD(5,2)	1

To find the quotient, use below function.

=QUOTIENT(5,2)	2

4.14 Find the value of x^y.

We can find the value of x^y using POWER function.

=POWER(2,2)	4

4.15 Finding the random numbers.

We can find the random numbers using below Formulae.

1. **Rand** function returns the random number between 0 and 1
2. **Randbetween** function returns the random integer number between given 2 values.

=RAND()	0.394094421
=RANDBETWEEN(1,100)	20

4.16 Rounding the numbers.

We can round the numbers using below Formulae in Excel.

1. ROUND
2. ROUNDDOWN
3. ROUNDUP
4. MROUND

ROUND function will round the number upto specified number of decimal in the second parameter. ROUNDUP and

ROUNDDOWN are 2 variants of the Round function. ROUNDUP function will round the number to the highest possible number. ROUNDDOWN function will round the number to the lowest possible number.

MROUND function will round the number to the nearest multiple of the second parameter.

As shown in the last example, MROUND(2.3,2) will produce the output as 2 as it is the multiple of 2 nearest to 2.3. MROUND(2.3,4) will produce the output as 4 as it is the multiple of 4 nearest to 2.3.

=ROUND(44.5354,2)	44.54
=ROUNDDOWN(44.657,2)	44.65
=ROUNDUP(44.657,2)	44.66
=MROUND(2.3,2)	2

4.17 Finding the sign of the number.

We can use SIGN function to get the sign of the number.

=SIGN(-22)	-1

4.18 Finding the square root of the number.

We can use SQRT function to get the square root of the number.

=SQRT(16)	4

4.19 Truncating the number.

We can truncate the number using below function.

=TRUNC(44.657,2)	44.65

4.20 Finding the SIN, COS.

We can use SIN and COS Formulae to find the SIN and COS of the degree.

=COS(0)	1
=SIN(0)	0

5. Lookup Formulae

5.1 Finding ADDRESS of the cell.

We can use Address function to find the address associated with any cell given its row and column number.

=ADDRESS(1,1)	A1

5.2 Finding the number of areas in given Range

AREAS function will return the total number of areas available in the given range.

=AREAS(B1:C4)	1

5.3 Selecting value from the array using index.

CHOOSE function will return the value in array at the given index. In below example, First parameter is 2. That means we have to get the value from the array at 2nd position which is equal to 22.

Please note that array can be any length and it can be a range.

=CHOOSE(2,11,22,33,44)	22

5.4 Finding the Row/Column number of given cell

ROW function is used to find the row of the given cell.

=ROW(A4)	4

COLUMN function is used to return the column number of the given cell.

=COLUMN(C33)	3

5.5 Finding the count of Rows/Columns in given range

We can find the total number of rows in the given range using ROWS function.

=ROWS(A2:E6)	5

We can find the total number of columns in the given range using COLUMNS function.

=COLUMNS(B33:C44)	2

5.6 HYPERLINK

HYPERLINK function is used to create the hyperlink in the cell. The first parameter is the url of the link and second parameter is the link text.

=HYPERLINK("http://www.google.com","go")	go

5.7 Finding the value in the array.

INDEX function is used to get the value at given row and column index from the array (Single or multi-dimensional array)

Single Dimensional Array

=INDEX(D1:D4,3,1)	33

Two Dimensional Array

=INDEX(D1:E4,3,2)	35

5.8 Searching a value in the array.

Match function is used to return the index at which given value is found in the array. In below example, we are trying to search 22 in the range D1:D4. Output is 2 that means 22 is present at D2.

=MATCH(22,D1:D4,0)	2

5.9 Get a value at the given offset relative to cell.

Offset function is used to find the value in the cell relative to other cell. In below example, we are trying to find the value in the cell that is 2 rows down and 2 columns right to the cell B1.

=OFFSET(B1,2,2)	33

5.10 Lookup Formulae

There are 3 kinds of Formulae in Excel.

1. LOOKUP
2. HLOOKUP
3. VLOOKUP

We can use look up Formulae to lookup the values in the range.

	A	B	C	D
1		Id	Name	Marks
2		111	sagar	44
3		222	amol	22
4		333	ganehs	33

Lookup function – Lookup function can be used to find the value in the last column in the array. In below example, we are looking up the value using 222. The value in the last column corresponding to this one is 22.

=LOOKUP(222,B1:D4)	22

Vlookup function –

Vlookup function is advanced version of the lookup function where in we can specify the column number from which we want the value. In below example, we are trying to find the value in the column number 3 for the record having ID 111.

=VLOOKUP(111,B1:D4,3)	44

Hlookup function –

For hlookup, consider below data.

	A	B	C	D
1	ID	11	22	33
2	Name	sagar	amol	ganesh
3	Marks	88	99	77

We can specify the row from where we want to find the value.In below example, we are trying to find the data from the row number 3, for the record whose ID is 22.

=HLOOKUP(22,A1:D3,3)	99

6. Logical Formulae

6.1 AND

We can use AND function to return true when all the conditions are true.

=AND(2<3,3>0,4)	TRUE
=AND(2<3,3>10,4)	FALSE

6.2 IF

IF function returns the first result if condition is true else it returns the second result.

=IF(2<3,"2 is less than 3","2 not less")	2 is less than 3

6.3 NOT

NOT function is used to get the reverse logical value.

=NOT(2<3)	FALSE
=NOT(2>3)	TRUE

6.4 OR

We can use OR function to return true when any one condition is true.

=OR(2<3,3>0,4)	TRUE
=OR(12<3,3>10,4=0)	FALSE

7. Information Formulae

7.1 Finding the information about Cell

We can find the information like contents, data type, row number, column number of the cell using CELL function as shown in below example.

=CELL("contents",A1)	Function
=CELL("type",A1)	l
=CELL("row",A2)	2

7.2 Check whether cell is blank.

We can see whether cell is blank using ISBLANK function. If the cell is blank, it returns true.

=ISBLANK(B2)	FALSE
=ISBLANK(C2)	TRUE

7.3 ISERROR Function.

We can see if the cell has an error using ISERROR function.

=ISERROR(B4)	FALSE

7.4 Checking for Even or Odd numbers.

We can check of the number is even or odd using ISEVEN and ISODD function respectively.

=ISEVEN(22)	TRUE
=ISEVEN(23)	FALSE

=ISODD(22)	FALSE
=ISODD(23)	TRUE

7.5 ISLOGICAL Function

We can check if the cell contains a logical value using ISLOGICAL function.

=ISLOGICAL(B14)	TRUE
=ISLOGICAL(B4)	FALSE

7.6 IsNA

We can check if the cell value is NA or not using ISNA function.

=ISNA(B4)	FALSE

7.7 Check if cell type is text.

ISTEXT function returns true if the cell value is textual.

ISNONTEXT function returns true if the cell value is non-textual.

=ISTEXT(E21)	TRUE
=ISTEXT(B20)	FALSE
=ISNONTEXT(E21)	FALSE
=ISNONTEXT(B20)	TRUE

7.8 Check if it is Number

We can check if the cell value is numerical using ISNUMBER function.

ISNUMBER function returns true if the cell value is numerical.

=ISNUMBER(D22)	TRUE
=ISNUMBER(D23)	FALSE

7.9 Get the data type of the Value in the cell.

We can get the data type of the cell value using TYPE function.

Below table shows the output of the function based upon the data type of the cell value.

IF VALUE IS	TYPE RETURNS
Number	1
Text	2
Logical value	4
Error value	16
Array	64

In below example, data type of cell D22 is Number. Data type of cell E21 is Text.

=TYPE(D22)	1
=TYPE(E21)	2

8. Statistical Formulae

8.1 Finding the Avarage of deviations

We can use AVEDEV function to find the average of deviations.

=AVEDEV(33,22,11)	7.333333333

8.2 Finding the Average of the numbers.

We can use AVERAGE function to find the average of the given numbers/range.

=AVERAGE(2,3,4)	3

8.3 Count numerical cells in given range

To find the cells in the given range having numerical values, we can use COUNT function.

As shown in below example, we have 2 cell in the range B1:B4 that have numbers in it.

=COUNT(B1:B4)	2

We can also count the cells based upon the conditions using COUNTIF function.

Below function will only count the cells having value greater than 1.

=COUNTIF(D1:D4,">4")	1

COUNTIFS function can be used to count the cell with multiple ranges and conditions.

=COUNTIFS(D1:D4,">4", E1:E4,">2")	4

8.4 Count Blank/Non-blank cells in given range

We can count the Non-blank cells in the given range using COUNTA function.

=COUNTA(B1:B4)	4

We can count the blank cells in the given range using COUNTBLANK function.

=COUNTBLANK(B1:B4)	3

8.5 Finding the min/max values in the given range.

We can find the minimum value in the given range using MIN function.

=MIN(2,3,4,5)	2

We can find the maximum value in the given range using MAX function.

=MAX(2,3,4,5)	5

8.6 Finding the median.

We can find the median of the given numbers using MEDIAN function.

=MEDIAN(2,3,4,5)	3.5

8.7 Finding the mode.

We can find the Mode of the given numbers using MODE function.

=MODE(2,3,4,5,3,4)	3

8.7 Finding the standard deviation.

We can find the standard deviation of the given numbers using STDEV function.

=STDEV(22,33,4,32)	13.45052663

8.8 Finding the Rank.

We can find the rank of the given number using RANK function.

=RANK(2,B12:B19,1)	3

8.9 The Subtotal Function

We can SUBTOTAL functio to perform aggregate operation on the arguments. The first parameter in the function specifies which operation has to be performed.

Below table gives idea about the significance of the 1st parameter.

If 1st parameter is 1, Average is returned. If it is 2, Count is returned and so on..

1ST PARAMETER VALUE (INCLUDES HIDDEN VALUES)	1ST PARAMETER VALUE (IGNORES HIDDEN VALUES)	OPERATION
1	101	AVERAGE
2	102	COUNT
3	103	COUNTA
4	104	MAX
5	105	MIN
6	106	PRODUCT
7	107	STDEV
8	108	STDEVP
9	109	SUM
10	110	VAR
11	111	VARP

For Example – to get the average of the values in the given range, you can use below function.

=SUBTOTAL(1,C68:F68)	27.5

To get the sum of the values in the given range, you can use below function.

=SUBTOTAL(9,C68:F68)	55

8.9 Finding the Sum.

We can find the sum of given range values using SUM function. To find the sum using some condition, we can use SUMIF function.

For example if the condition is <100, that means SUMIF function will return the sum of the numbers in the range that are less than 100.

We can use SUMSQ function to get the sum of the squares of the arguments.

=SUM(22,11,4,5.5)	42.5
=SUMIF(D55:D60,"<100")	33
=SUMSQ(2,3,4)	29

9. Engineering Formulae

9.1 Converting Decimal Numbers

Excel provides 3 Formulae to convert the decimal values to binary, hexadecimal and octal as shown below.

=DEC2BIN(12)	1100
=DEC2HEX(12)	C
=DEC2OCT(12)	14

9.2 Converting HexaDecimal Numbers

Excel provides 3 Formulae to convert the hexadecimal values to binary, decimal and octal as shown below.

=HEX2BIN("1F")	11111
=HEX2DEC("1F")	31
=HEX2OCT("1F")	37

9.3 Converting Binary Numbers

Excel provides 3 Formulae to convert the binary values to decimal, hexadecimal and octal as shown below.

=BIN2DEC(1001)	9

=BIN2HEX(11111)	1F
=BIN2OCT(1111)	17

9.4 Converting Octal Numbers

Excel provides 3 Formulae to convert the octal values to binary, hexadecimal and decimal as shown below.

=OCT2BIN(14)	1100
=OCT2HEX(14)	C
=OCT2DEC(14)	12

9.5 Working with Complex numbers

We can perform operation on complex number in excel using variuos Formulae.

COMPLEX function is used to create the complex number out of 2 parameters as shown below.

=COMPLEX(3,2)	3+2i

To find the sum of 2 numbers, you can use below function.

=IMSUM("2+3i","4+4i")	6+7i

To subtract 2 complex numbers, you can use below function.

=IMSUB("2+3i","4+4i")	-2-i

To find the product of 2 complex numbers, you can use below function.

=IMPRODUCT("2+3i","4+4i")	-4+20i

9.6 Converting Units (Distance, Mass, Time)

To convert the number from one measurement system to another, we can use CONVERT function.

Below function will convert 1miles to meters.

=CONVERT(1,"mi","m")	1609.344

In the similar way we can convert the numbers into other distance units like inch(in), foot(ft), yard(yd) etc

Below function will convert 1 year to days.

=CONVERT(1,"yr","day")	365.25

In similar way, you can convert time units to hour(hr), minute(mn), second(sec) etc.

Below function will convert the gram to slug. In the same way, you can convert it to other system like Pound mass (lbm), atomic mass unit(U), Ounce mass (ozm).

=CONVERT(8000,"g","sg")	0.548174127

We can convert the pressure units as mentioned below.

=CONVERT(1,"Pa","mmHg")	0.007500617

For power units, you can see below example.

We have converted 1 horse power to watt.

=CONVERT(1,"HP","w")	745.6998716

We can convert the tempreature in Fahrenheit to celcius as shown in below example.

=CONVERT(100,"F","C")	37.77777778

We can also convert energy units as mentioned below.

We have converted 1 Joule to Calories.

=CONVERT(1,"J","c")	0.239005736

10. Financial Formulae

10.1 Loan related Formulae.

We have 3 Formulae related to the loan.

1. PMT – to find the EMI (Fixed monthly payments)
2. RATE – to find the interest rate
3. IPMT – to find the interest component of the EMI.

=PMT(10.5%/12,12*30,2230000)	Rs. -20,398.69
=RATE(12*30,-20398.69000,2230000)*12	11%
=IPMT(10.5%/12,1,12*30,2230000)	Rs. -19,512.50

There are other Formulae that can be used to calculate security related payments.

11. Database Formulae

To understand database Formulae, we will consider below data. There are 3 columns in the table. First 2 rows are used to specify the filter conditions.
Row 3 to 7 contains actual table header and data.

	A	B	C
1	id	name	marks
2	<3		
3	id	name	marks
4	1	sagar	43
5	2	amol	55
6	3	susan	32
7	4	billy	64

11.1 DMIN

This function is used to find the minimum value in the column. This function takes 3 parameters.

1. 1st parameter is used to specify the data
2. 2nd parameter is used to specify the column
3. 3rd parameter is used to specify the filters

=DMIN(A3:C7,"marks",A1:C2)	43

The output is 43 as we have a filter that id < 3.

11.2 DMAX

This function is used to find the maximum value in the column.

This function is similar to DMIN from parameter perspective.

=DMAX(A3:C7,"marks",A1:C2)	55

11.3 DCOUNT

This function returns the count of matching records.

This function is similar to DMIN from parameter perspective.

=DCOUNT(A3:C7,"marks",A1:C2)	2

11.4 DAvarage

This function finds the average of the values in the column.

=DAVERAGE(A3:C7,"marks",A1:C2)	49

12. User Defined Formulae

So far we have seen the built-in Formulae of excel. We can also write our own Formulae in excel using VBA programming. It is also called as macros.

In this chapter you will learn about below topics.

1. Visual basic editor features in Excel.
2. Record new macro
3. Debug a macro
4. Run a Macro.
5. Basic VBA programming
6. Modules
7. Sub procedures
8. Function.

12.1 Recording excel macros

Before I tell you how to record macros, let me explain how to show developer Tab in Excel 2010.

On the menubar, you have to right click and then you will see below context menu. Click on Customize the ribbon.

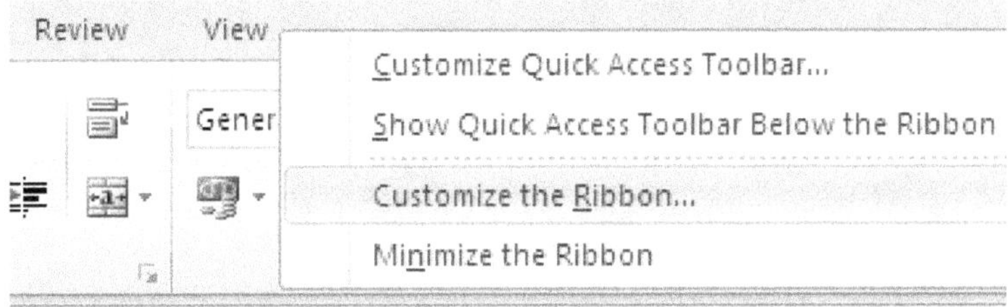

Figure 1 - Customize Ribbon

After this, you will see ribbon dialog window. It will show the main tabs as displayed in below figure. You have to select the checkbox in front of the Developer tab and then click on Ok

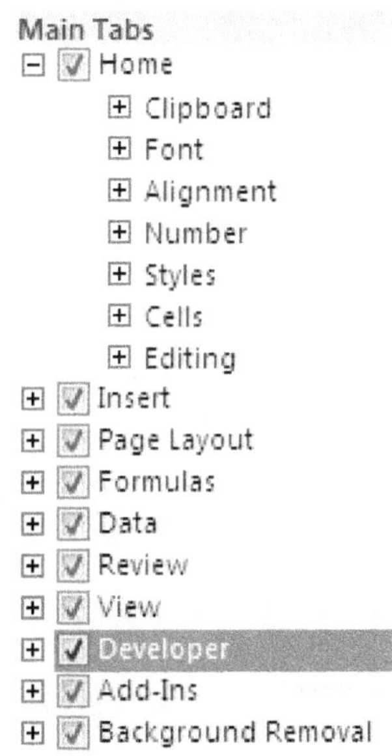

Figure 2 - Select Developer Tab

After you click on ok button, developer tab will be shown in Excel menu bar as shown in below figure.

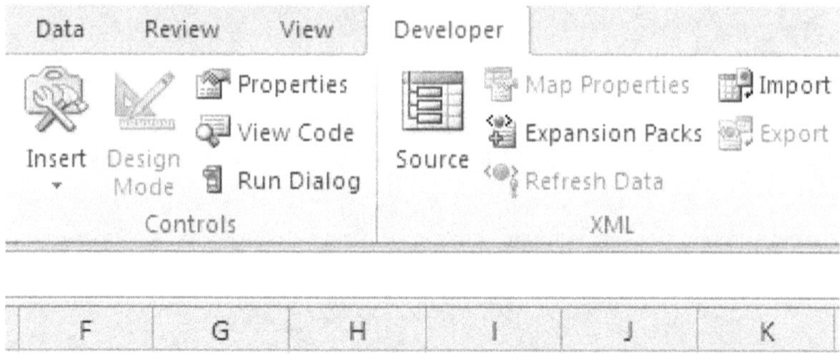

Figure 3 - Developer Tab

When you click on the developer tab, you will see below command group at the left side. To record a new macro , you will have to click on – "Record Macro" command button.

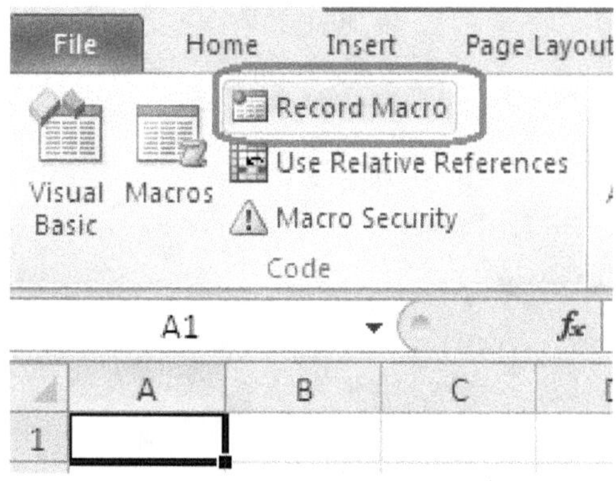

Figure 4 - Record Macro Button

Next below dialog window will open asking you the details of the macro you will be recording

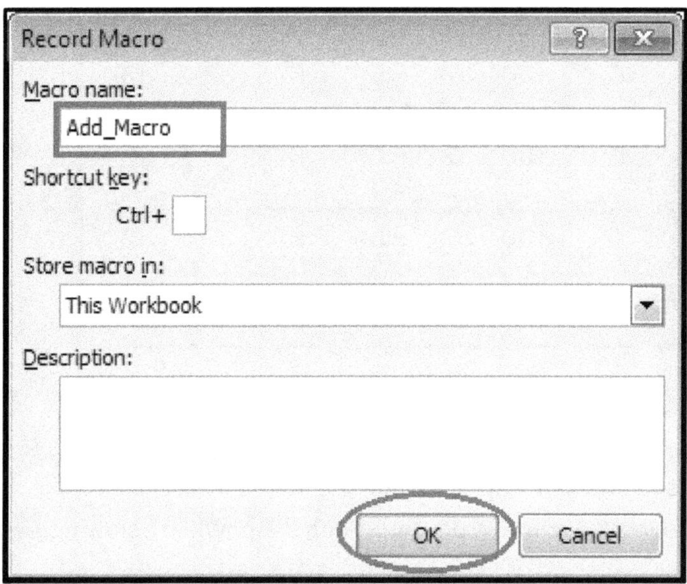

You will have to provide the name of macro. You can also assign the shortcut key to macro. You can store the macro in current workbook or any other workbook as well. Finally you have to give the description of the macro. Please note that your macro name should not contain blank spaces and other special characters like $#@!

After you click on the ok button, macro recording starts. Whatever operation you do on excel sheet will be recorded and macro code will be created automatically.

For the simplicity, I am going to perform addition of values in the cells A3 and B3. The sum of these 2 values will be stored in the cell - C3 as displayed in below figure. But if you want, you can perform any complex calaculations while recording. You can even add charts as well.

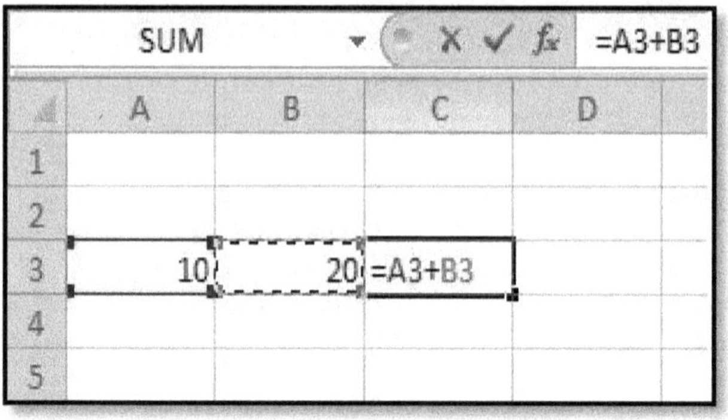

Figure 5 - Recording Macro

After this you can stop recording the macro by clicking on the button displayed in the developer tab as shown in below figure.

That's all. You have just created new macro in excel.

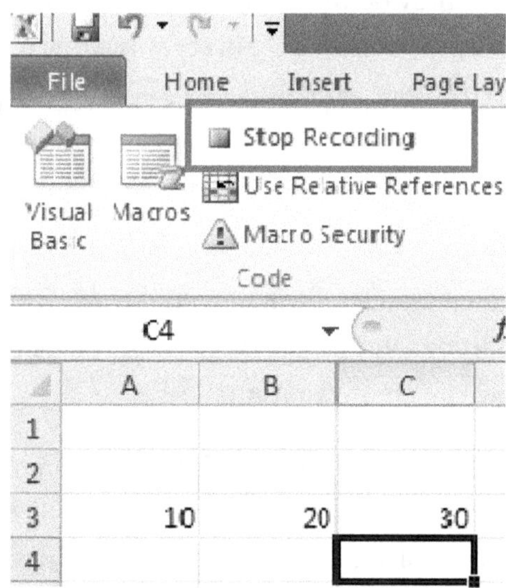

Figure 6 - Stop recording

12.2 View and Run excel macro.

You can view excel macro by clicking the macros button displayed near record button.

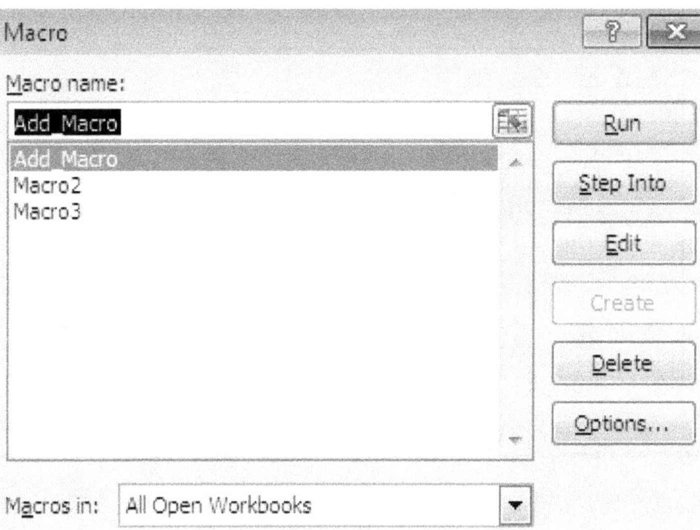

Figure 7 - View Macros

As shown in above figure, You will be able to see all macros in open workbooks. On the right hand side, you will be able to see buttons to run, debug, edit, delete buttons. To run the macro, just click on the Run button. All operations that you performed while recording will be done automatically. To view the macro code you can click on edit button.

12.3 Debugging the excel macro.

When you click on the edit button in previuos window, you will see the macro code as shown in below figure. You can debug the code to see how the macro performs each operation in sequence. You can also find the errors in the macro by debugging it.

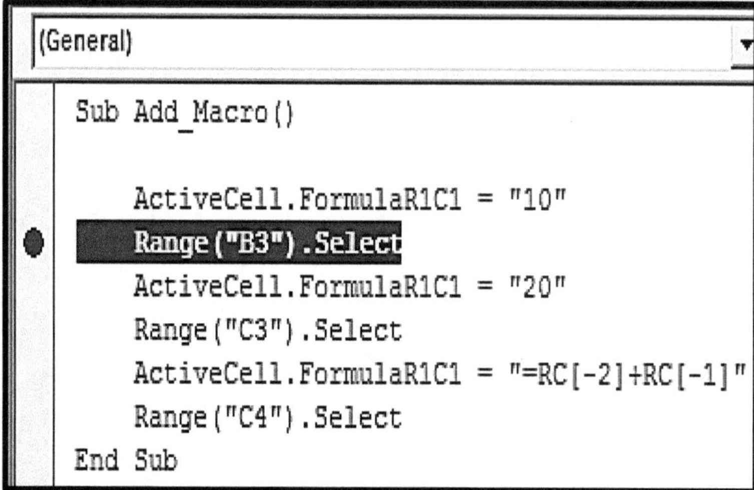

Figure 8 - Debug the macro

To add breakpoint, you have to click on the vertical bar in front of the line of code. When you run the macro, control will pause at the breakpoint and from there you can execute your code line by line using F8 key.

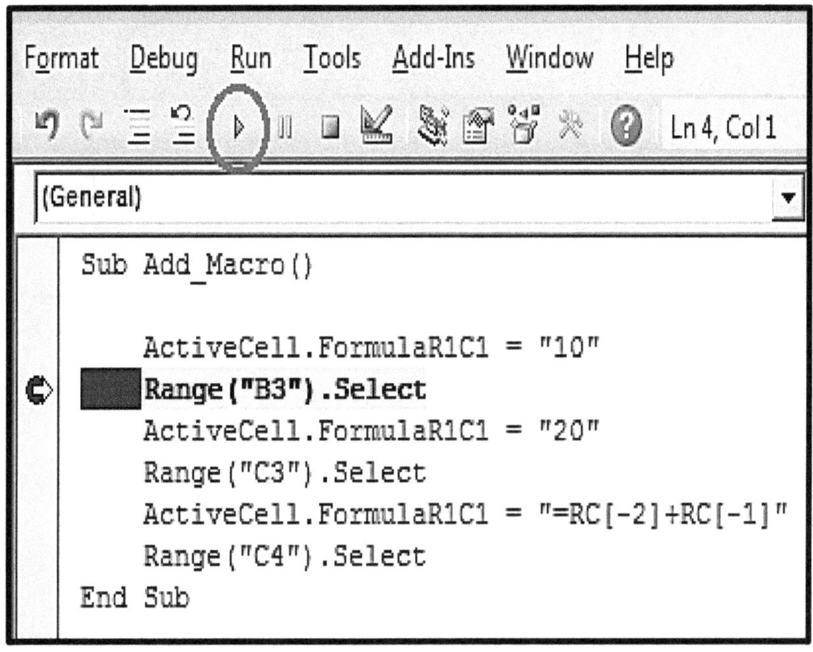

Figure 9 - Macro control pauses at breakpoint

12.4 Visual Basic Editor

You can open visual basic editor by clicking on the visual basic command button as shown in below figure.

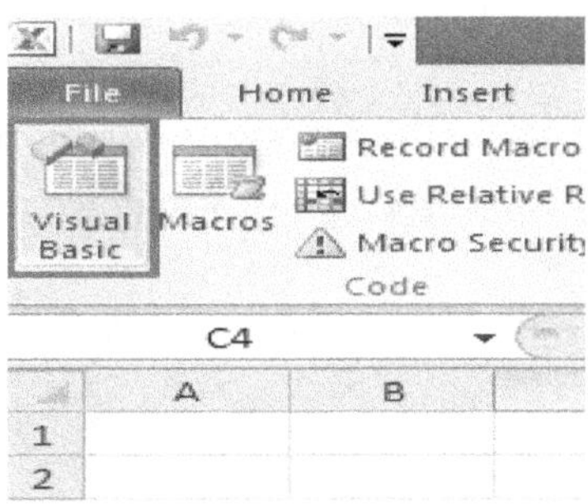

Figure 10 – Open Visual Basic Editor

Visual basic editor window will show you excel sheet objects, modules and macros in the workbook as shown in below figure.

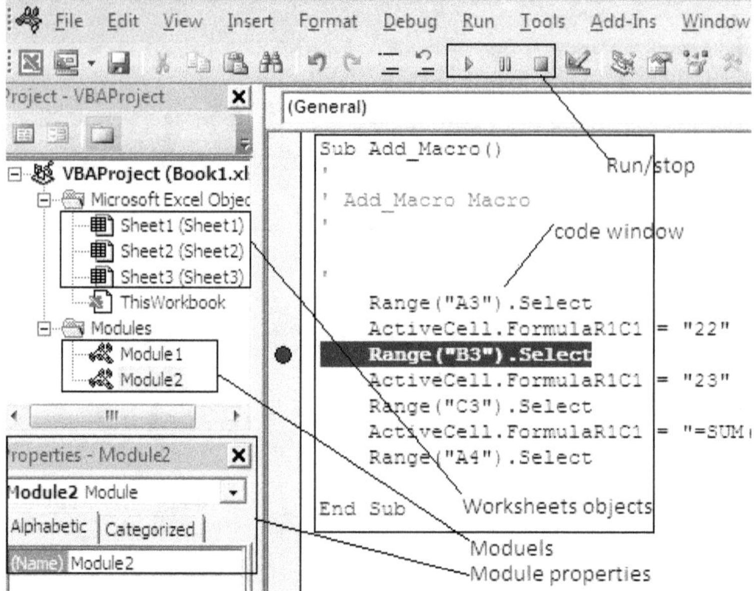

Figure 11 - VB Editor in Excel

We have below windows in VBA Editor that can be used while running macro.

1. Watch Window
2. Immediate Window
3. Locals Window

These 3 windows help us in debugging the macro. In watch window, we can inspect the variables value.

Let us have a look at each window.

Watch Window

To see the value of the variable, in the debug mode you have to right click on it and then select add to watch. As seen in next figure, I have added variable a to the watch window and the value of a is 20 .

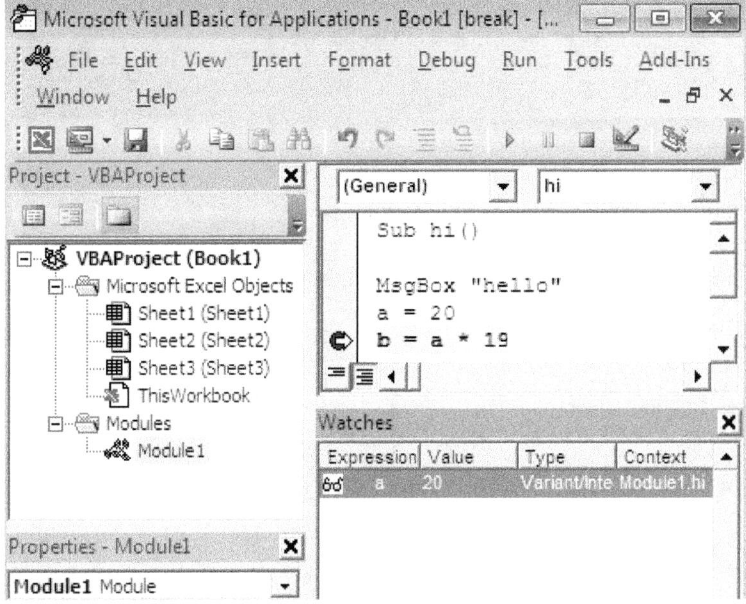

Figure 12 - Watch Window in VBA Editor

Immediate Window

We can use immediate window to see the output of the macro as shown in next figure. The debug.print statement will print the value |23 in the immediate window. This is how we can monitor if our program is producing correct output or not.

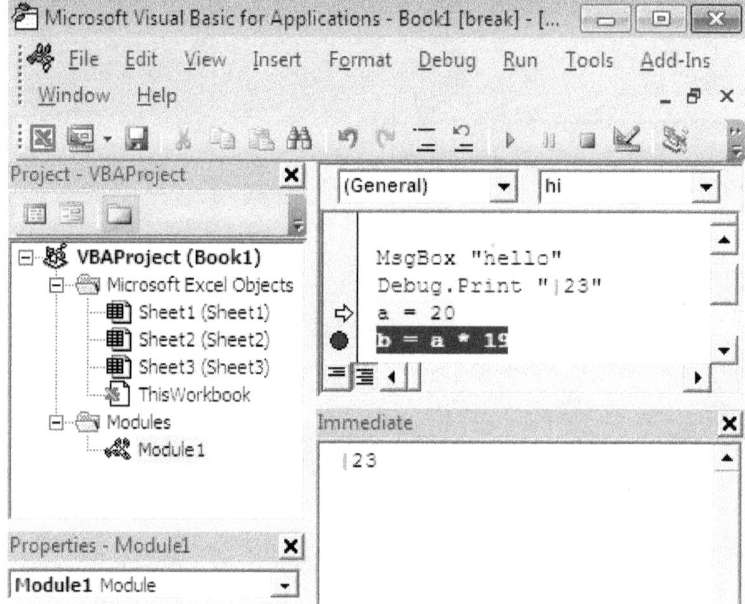

Figure 13 - Immediate Window in VBA Editor

Locals Window

We can use Locals window to see the values of local variables. As shown in next figure, we have a locals window showing the values of variables a and b. Locals window is also showing the data type of these variables.

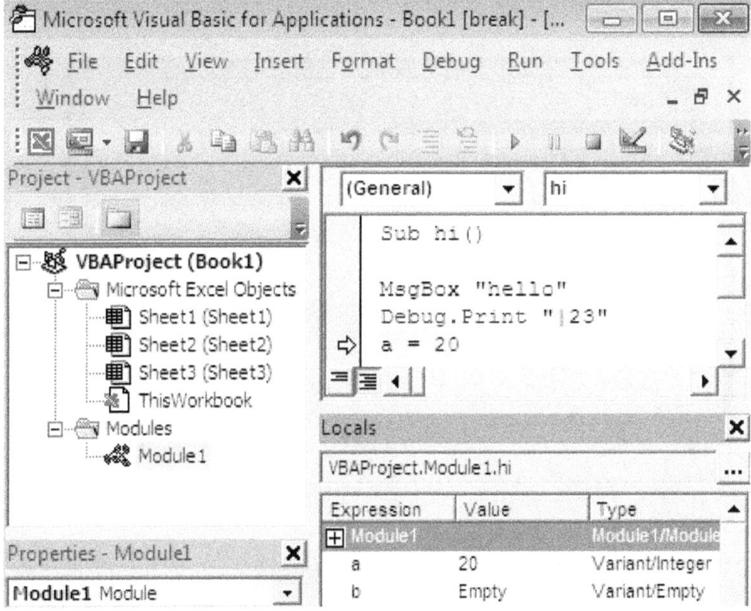

Figure 14 - Locals Window in VBA Editor

12.5 Modules in VBA

Modules are used to store the macros together. We can group similar macros in a separate module for easy reference.

Actually when you record a macro, that macro code is stored in the modules.

12.6 Sub routines in VBA

Sub routines are nothing but macro procedures. They are used to increase the reusability of the code. You can call the same sub procedure any number of time to perform specific task.

For example in below figure, there is one macro or sub procedure called Add_Macro.

```
(General)
Sub Add_Macro()

Set WB = Workbooks.Add
 WB.Title = "New WB"
 WB.SaveAs Filename:="D:\F1.xls"

End Sub
```

12.7 Functions in VBA

Functions are similar to the sub procedures. Only the difference is that functions return a value while procedure does not return a value.

Function Example

In below example, I have created one function called add which takes 2 input values a and b. Then it adds 2 numbers and returns the sum to calling sub – sample.

```
Sub sample()

      x = add(2, 3)
```

```
    MsgBox x
End Sub
Function add(a, b)
    add = a + b
End Function
```

12.8 User Forms in VBA

VBA editor also provides the feature called user forms which can be used to create the interactive user forms.

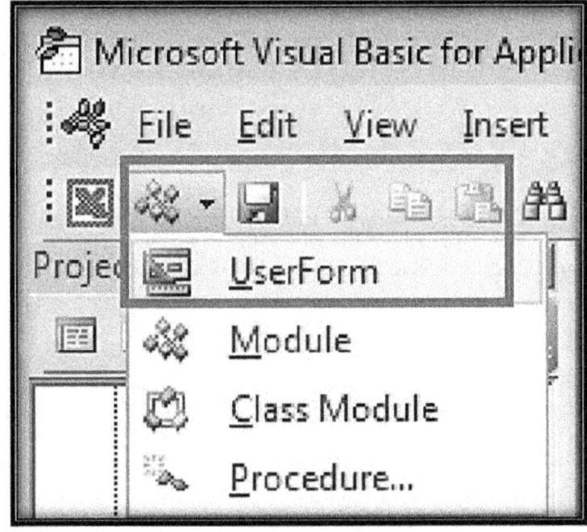

Figure 15 - User Forms in VBA

When you add user form to the VBA project, you will see new user form in design mode. You will also see the toolbox showing common form controls like command button, checkbox, radiobutton, textbox, combobox etc.

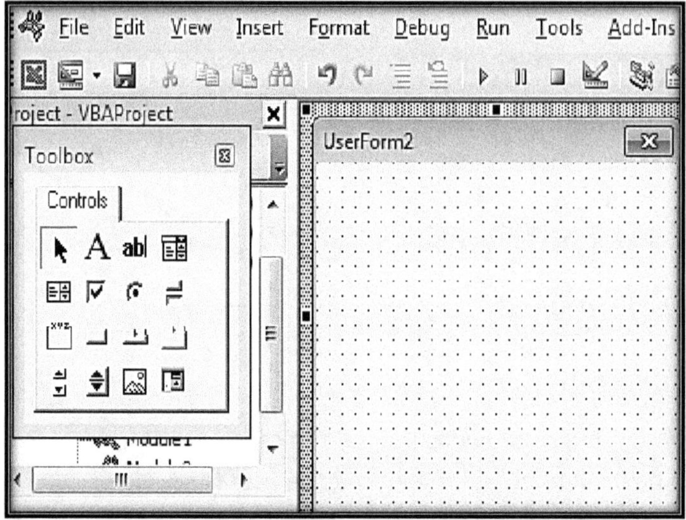

You can create windows based applications using user forms. For example – You can add command button in the form and then call a macro on button click event.

12.9 Events in VBA

VBA is an event driven programming language. All important excel objects like worksheets and workbooks support events.

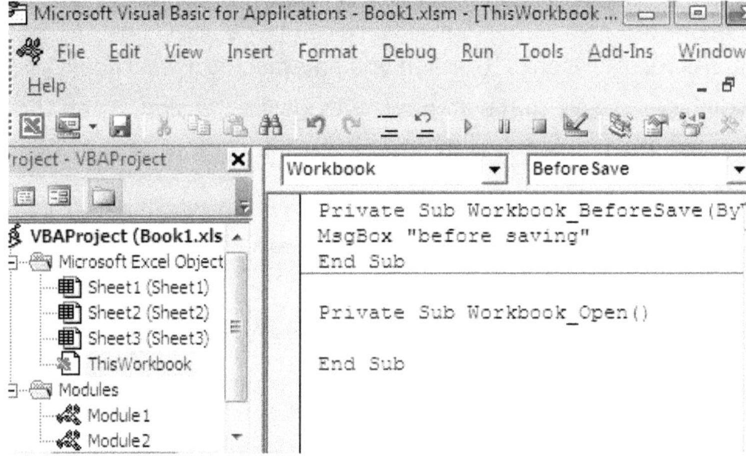

When you double click on the worksheet or workbook object you can see what all events that object support.

For example – As shown in previous figure, you can see events supported by workbook. Second combobox contains all events. When you select new event from the dropdown, the code for that event is automatically added in the code window.

In below code, I have added code which will execute when you try to save the current workbook.

```
Private Sub Workbook_BeforeSave(ByVal
SaveAsUI As Boolean, Cancel As Boolean)

      MsgBox "before saving"

End Sub
```

12.10 Saving excel macro workbooks

In Microsoft Excel 2010, when you add macro to workbook, you will have to save that workbook with **xlsm** extension. If you try to save the workbook with other extension, you will get below error.

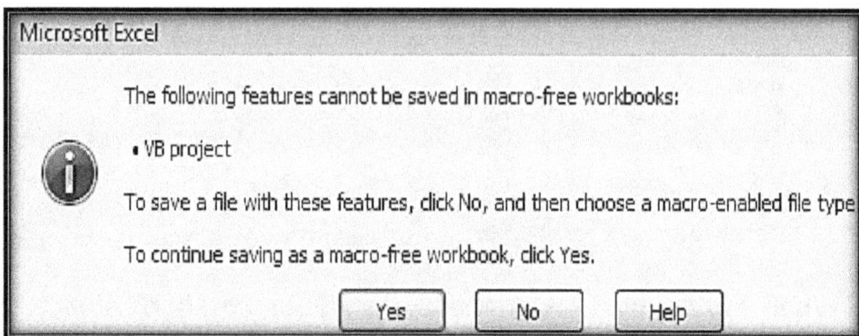

12.11 Enabling excel macro.

When you try to open excel workbook which contains macros, you may see below message saying that macros may contain viruses or other securtiy hazards. Do not enable this content unless you trust th esource of this file.

You will also see 2 buttons – enable macros and disable macros. If you know the source of the excel file and you really want to use macros, then only you should click on enable macros button. Otherwise it is good practise to click on disable macros.

12.12 Understanding Trust Center settings

Trust Center provides important settings related to macros. To open trust center you will have to follow below steps.

1. Click on options in File Menu.
2. In Excel options window, click on Trust Center.
3. There you will have to click on Trust Center settings button.
4. Trust Center window Opens.

As you can see in next figure, trust center has important settings related to the macro like

1. Trusted Publishers.
2. Trusted Locations.
3. Trusted Documents.
4. Macro Settings

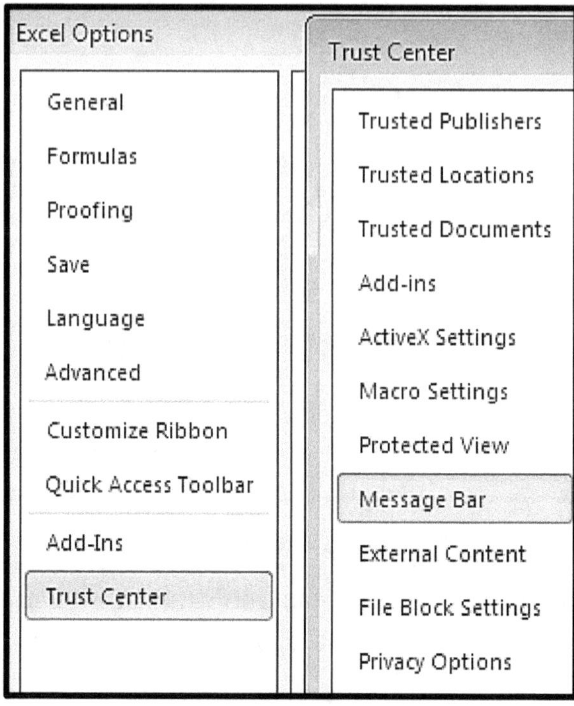

Figure 16 - Trust Center Settings

12.13 Adding Macros to the toolbar

As I said earlier,we can execute the macros by going to developer tab and then clicking on macros buttons, you will see all macros.

You can also run the macro by adding a command to toolbar. You will have to follow below steps to creat a macro command button.

1. Open a cutomize ribbon window.
2. From left side drop down, select macros option
3. Create a custom command group.
4. Add macro that you want to show on toolbar.

Below figure shows how we can do it.

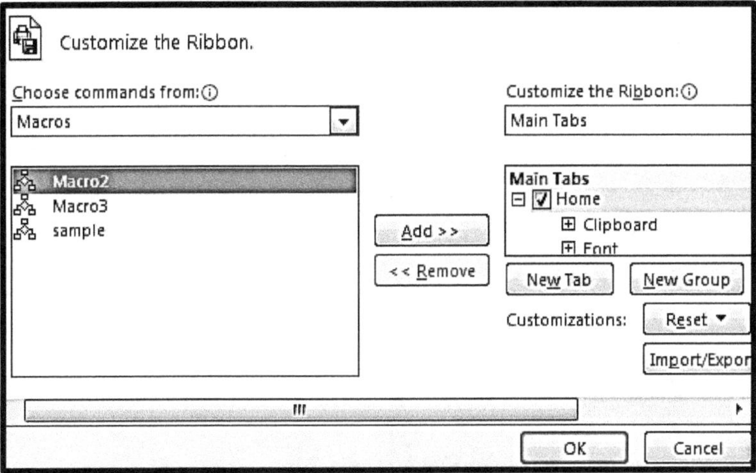

Figure 17 - Adding the macro to toolbar

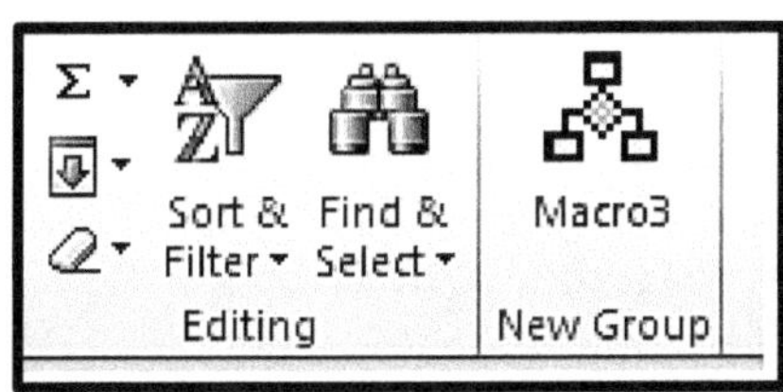

Figure 18 - Macro added to toolbar

As you can see in above figure, I have added macro 3 to the custom command group in Home tab. You can execute that macro by just clicking on it.

13. VBA(Macro) Programming Concepts

This is the most important chapter. In this chapter, you will learn basic concepts in VBA language like....

13.1 Variables and data types in VBA

Variables are used to store the data in the program. It is not mandatory to declare the variables in VBA. The data type of the variable changes as per the type of data we store in that variable.

<u>Variables Declaration</u>

Syntax:-

Dim VariableName As Data Type

For Example

```
Dim no As Integer
Dim str1 As String
Dim c As Characters
```

<u>Variables initialization</u>

```
Dim str As String
str = "String name"
```

Variables are of 2 types.

1. Scalar – stores one value at a time
2. Array – stores multiple values at a time

VBA has mainly 2 types of Data Types – numeric and non-numeric..

1. Numeric
2. Non - Numeric

Numeric Data Types

Type	Storage	Range of Values
Byte	1 Byte	0 to 255
Integer	2 bytes	-32,768 to 32,767
Long	4 bytes	-2,147,483,648 to 2,147,483,648
Single	4 bytes	-3.402823E+38 to -1.401298E-45 for negative values 1.401298E-45 to 3.402823E+38 for positive values.
Double	8 bytes	-1.79769313486232e+308 to - 4.94065645841247E-324 for negative values 4.94065645841247E-324 to 1.79769313486232e+308 for positive values.
Currency	8 bytes	-922,337,203,685,477.5808 to 922,337,203,685,477.5807
Decimal	12 bytes	+/- 79,228,162,514,264,337,593,543,950,335 if no decimal is use +/- 7.9228162514264337593543950335 (28 decimal places)

Non-Numeric Data Types

Data Type	Storage	Range
String(fixed length)	Length of string	1 to 65,400 characters
String(variable length	Length + 10 bytes	0 to 2 billion characters
Date	8 bytes	January 1, 100 to December 31, 9999
Boolean	2 bytes	True or False
Object	4 bytes	Any embedded objec
Variant(numeric	16 bytes	Any value as large as Double
Variant(text)	Length+22 bytes	Same as variable-length string

13.2 Control statements (Conditional and loop)

VBA has 2 kinds of conditional statements.

1. If ..then ..else
2. Select ...case

1) If...Then ...Else

```
Sub condition()
   Dim a As Integer
   Dim b As Integer
    a = 10
    b = 15
  If (a > b) Then
     MsgBox "a is grater"
  Else
     MsgBox "b is grater"

  End If

End Sub
```

2) Select case

```
Sub Selectcase()
    Dim a As Integer
    Dim b As Integer
    Dim c As Integer

      a = 10
      b = 15

    Select Case (3)
      Case 1
        c = a + b
        MsgBox (c)
      Case 2
        c = a - b
        MsgBox (c)
      Case 3
```

```
        c = a * b
        MsgBox (c)
    End Select

End Sub
```

VBA has 2 kinds of loop statements.

1. Do While..loop
2. For loop

3) Do While...Loop

```
Sub Whileloop()

    Dim i As Integer
    i = 1
    Dim str As String
      str = "Computer"
    Do While i <= 10

        Cells(i, 2).Value = str
         i = i + 1
    Loop

End Sub
```

Output:

E13			
	A	B	C
1		Computer	
2		Computer	
3		Computer	
4		Computer	
5		Computer	
6		Computer	
7		Computer	
8		Computer	
9		Computer	
10		Computer	
11			

4) For....Next loop

```
Sub Forloop()

    Dim i As Integer

    For i = 1 To 10
      Cells(i, 1).Value = i
    Next

End Sub
```

Output:

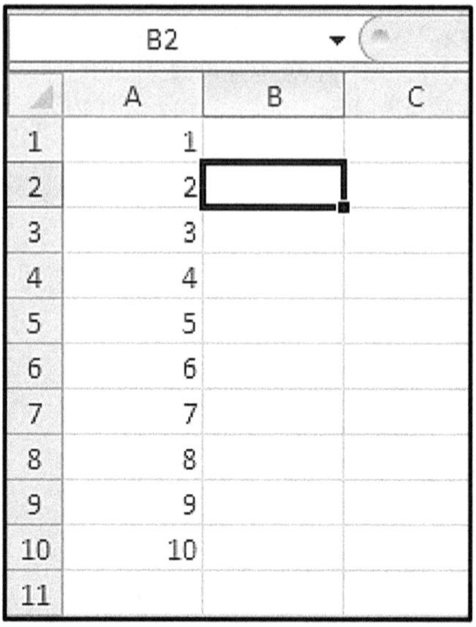

B2

	A	B	C
1	1		
2	2		
3	3		
4	4		
5	5		
6	6		
7	7		
8	8		
9	9		
10	10		
11			

13.3 String functions in VBA

String functions are used to perform various operations on the text values in VBA. Below example will demonstrate all string function in VBA.

```
Sub Stringfunction()

    Dim str As String

    'to get the position of a substring
Cells(1, 1).Value = "sagar salunke "
    str = Cells(1, 1).Value
    Cells(3, 2) = InStr(str, "p")

    'to extract substring from the left
    Cells(4, 2) = Left(str, 4)

    'to extract substring from the right
    Cells(5, 2) = Right(str, 5)
```

```
    'to get the middle part of string
    Cells(6, 2) = Mid(str, 3, 7)

    'to get the length of a string
    str = Cells(1, 1).Value
    Cells(7, 2) = Len(str)

    'to Convert the string to lower case
    Cells(8, 2) = LCase(str)

    'to Convert the string to upper
    Cells(9, 2) = UCase(str)

     'to trim the string
    Cells(10, 2) = Trim(str)

    'to trim the string from left

    Cells(11, 2) = LTrim(str)

    'to trim the string from right

    Cells(12, 2) = RTrim(str)

    'to Replace the string

    Cells(13, 2) = Replace("This is a ",
"a", "computer")

    'to Reverse the string
    str = Cells(1, 1).Value
    Cells(14, 2) = StrReverse(str)



    'to Compare two strings
    Cells(16, 2) = StrComp(str, "macro")
```

```
End Sub
```

	A	B
1	sagar salunke	
2		
3	instr	0
4	left	saga
5	right	unke
6	mid	gar sal
7	length	14
8	lcase	sagar salunke
9	ucase	SAGAR SALUNKE
10	trim	sagar salunke
11	ltrim	sagar salunke
12	rtrim	sagar salunke
13	replace	This is computer
14	reverse	eknulas ragas

Figure 19 - String Function Output

13.4 Date and Time functions in VBA

We can perform date and time operations easily using below functions

1. Now – gets current system timestamp
2. Date – gets current system date
3. DateAdd – adds interval to date
4. DateDiff – finds the difference between 2 dates.

1)DateAdd Example

Syntax:- DateAdd(interval,number,date)

The interval you want to add

- yyyy -Year
- q -Quarter
- m -Month
- y - Day of year
- d -Day
- w -Weekday
- ww - Week of year
- h -Hour
- n -Minute
- s –Second

```
Sub Addatefunction()

    'return the current date and time
    Cells(3, 2) = Now

    'Return the current date
    Cells(4, 2) = Date

    'Add Year
    Cells(4,2)=(DateAdd("yyyy",2,Date))

    'Add Month
    Cells(5, 2)=(DateAdd("m", 2, Date))

    'Add day
    Cells(6, 2)=(DateAdd("d", 2, Date))

    'Add Weekday
    Cells(7, 2)=(DateAdd("w", 8, Date))

    'Add Week of year
    Cells(8, 2)=(DateAdd("ww", 2, Date))

    'Add Hours
```

```
    Cells(9, 2) = (DateAdd("h", 1, Now))

    'Add Minutes
    Cells(10,2)=(DateAdd("n",1 Now))

    'Add Seconds
    Cells(11, 2) = (DateAdd("s",1,Now))


End Sub
```

2) DateDiff Example

```
Sub Datedifffunction()

firstDate = "11-Mar-14 00:00:00"
secondDate = "31-Mar-15 23:59:00"

Cells(3,2)=CStr(DateDiff("yyyy",
fDate,tDate))
Cells(4, 2) = (DateDiff("q", firstDate,
secondDate))

Cells(5, 2) = (DateDiff("m", firstDate,
secondDate))

Cells(6, 2) = (DateDiff("h", firstDate,
secondDate))

Cells(7, 2) = (DateDiff("w", firstDate,
secondDate))

Cells(8, 2) = (DateDiff("s", firstDate,
secondDate))
```

```
Cells(9, 2) = (DateDiff("ww", firstDate,
secondDate))

Cells(10, 2) = (DateDiff("y", firstDate,
secondDate))

Cells(11, 2) = (DateDiff("d", firstDate,
secondDate))

Cells(12, 2) = (DateDiff("n", firstDate,
secondDate))

End Sub
```

Output:-

	A	B	C
1			
2	Difference		
3	Year	1	
4	Quarter	4	
5	Months	12	
6	Hour	9263	
7	Weekday	55	
8	Second	33350340	
9	Week of y	55	
10	Day of yea	385	
11	Day	385	
12	Minute	555839	
13			

Figure 20-Datediff

3) DatePart

```
Sub Datepartfunction()

   'return the date
   d = CDate("2010-02-16")
   Cells(3, 2) = (DatePart("d", d))

    'Return month
   d = CDate("2010-02-16")
   Cells(4, 2) = (DatePart("m", d))

    'Return Year
   d = CDate("2010-02-16")
   Cells(5, 2) = (DatePart("yyyy", d))

    'Return Hours
```

```
    Cells(6, 2) = (DatePart("h", Now()))

     'Return Minutes
    Cells(7, 2) = (DatePart("n", Now()))

     'Return Seconds
    Cells(8, 2) = (DatePart("s", Now()))

End Sub
```

Output :-

	A	B	C
1			
2	**DatePart is**		
3	Date	16	
4	Month	2	
5	Year	2010	
6	Hours	17	
7	Minutes	3	
8	Seconds	53	
9			
10			

4) DateSerial

Syntax:- DateSerial(year,month,day)

```
Sub Dateserialfunction()


Cells(3,2)=CDate(DateSerial(2014,3,27))
```

```
    'Subtract 15 days:
  Cells(4,2)=(DateSerial(2014,3,6-15))

    'Add 5 Days
  Cells(5,2)=(DateSerial(2014,3,6+5))

End Sub
```

Output:-

	A	B	C
1			
2	**DateSerial**		
3	Print serial	27-03-2014	
4	Subtract 15 days	19-02-2014	
5	Add 5 days	11-03-2014	
6			
7			
8			
9			

5) DateValue

```
Sub Datevaluefunction()

  Cells(8,2)=(DateValue("27-Mar-14"))

End Sub
```

Output:-

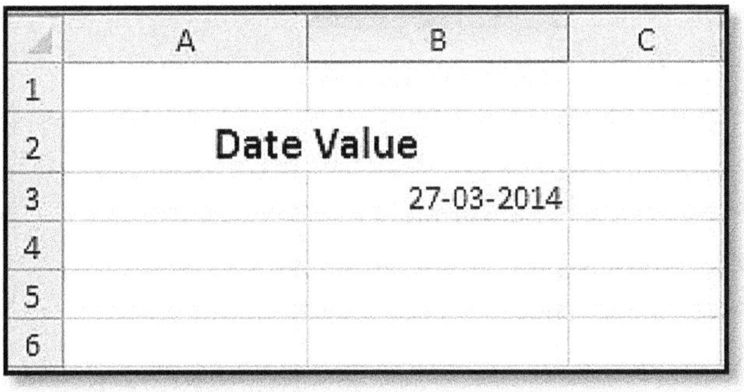

	A	B	C
1			
2	Date Value		
3		27-03-2014	
4			
5			
6			

6) FormatDateTime

```
Sub Formatdatefun()

   Cells(3,2)=(FormatDateTime(Now()))
   Cells(4,2)=(FormatDateTime(Now(),1))
   Cells(5,2)=(FormatDateTime(Now(),2))
   Cells(6,2)=(FormatDateTime(Now(),3))
   Cells(7,2)=(FormatDateTime(Now(),4))

End Sub
```

Output :-

	A	B	C
1			
2	**Format date time**		
3	Current datetim	27-03-2014 17:24:38	
4	Long date	27-Mar-14	
5	Short date	27-03-2014	
6	long time	17:24:38	
7	short time	17:24	
8			
9			

7) IsDate

IsDate function returns the True Or False

```
Sub Isdatefun()

    Cells(3,2)=(IsDate("April 22,1947"))

    Cells(6,2)=(IsDate("52/17/2010"))

    Cells(4,2)=(IsDate(#1/31/2010#))

    Cells(5,2)=(IsDate("#01/31/10#"))

End Sub
```

Output :-

	A	B
1		
2	**IsDate**	
3		TRUE
4		TRUE
5		FALSE
6		FALSE
7		
8		
9		

8) WeekdayName

```
Sub Weekdayfun()

    Cells(3, 2) = (WeekdayName(5))

End Sub
```

13.5 Math functions in VBA

Important Math functions in VBA are given below.

1. Round – finds the round value of the number
2. Abs – finds the absolute value
3. Sqrt – finds square root of the number
4. ^ - finds x^y

```
Sub Weekdayfun()

 x = 2 ^ 3
   MsgBox x
    'prints 8

```

```
    MsgBox Round(33.243, 2)
    'prints 33.24

    MsgBox Abs(-23.22)
    'prints 23.22

    MsgBox Sqr(4)
    'prints 2

    MsgBox (Exp(5.5))
    'print 244.69193226422

    MsgBox (Int(4.4567))
    'print 4

    MsgBox (Tan(55))
    'print -45.1830879105211

    MsgBox (Rnd)
    'print 0.5795186

End Sub
```

13.6 Excel object model in VBA

Excel Application is built using object oreinted programming paradigm. So everything is object in Excel. . To view all objects in Excel you can click on object browser button in VBA as shown in below figure

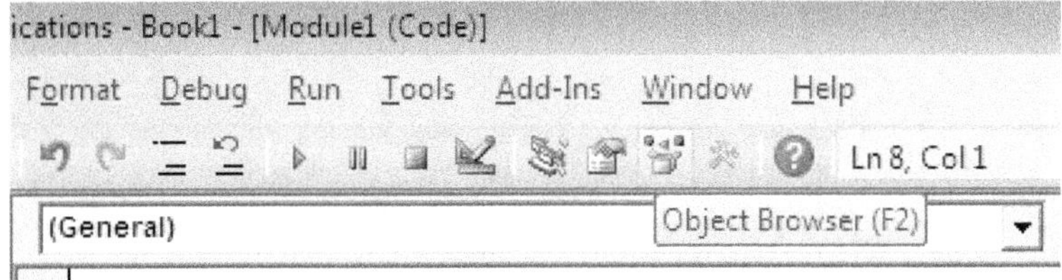

Figure 21 - Click on the Object Browser Button

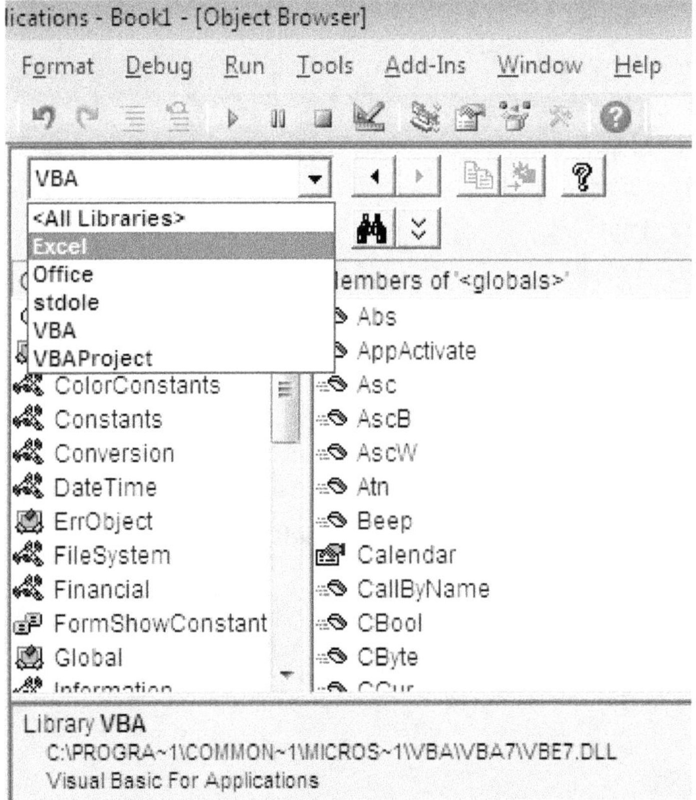

Figure 22 - View Excel library Objects

Then you can select Excel library from the dropdown to view all objects as shown in the above figure. To return to code window, you will have to press F7.

List of important objects and collections in Excel is given below.

1. Application
2. Workbook
3. Worksheet
4. Range
5. Workbooks
6. Worksheets
7. Shape
8. Chart
9. Font
10. Border
11. Comment

14. Automating Workbooks using macros.

In this chapter you will learn about automating the workbook tasks using macros like....

1. Creating and saving new workbook
2. Deleteing existing workbook
3. Opening and reading a workbook
4. Protecting workbook

14.1 Creating a new workbook

Below Code/Example can be used to create a new Excel workbook and save it using VBA Macro.
Syntax and Example of VBA Macro to Create a new workbook.

```
Sub AddNewWorkbook()

 Set WB = Workbooks.Add
 WB.Title = "New WB"
 WB.SaveAs Filename:="D:\F1.xls"

End Sub
```

Above code will create a new workbook with title as New WB and It will Save the new Workbook to location @ D:\F1.xls

14.2 Delete a workbook

We can use below macro code to delete a workbook. The first line in the code creates the file system object. Then we have used deletefile method to delete a workbook stored at d:\f1.xls.

```
Set fso =
CreateObject("scripting.filesystemobject")

fso.deletefile ("d:\f1.xls")
```

14.3 Open a workbook

We can use below macro code to open a workbook. The first line in the code will open the workbook located at location d:\f1.xls. Then we have stored a value 22 in the cell A1. Then we have used save method and closed the workbook using close method

```
Sub Open_Workbook()

Set wb=
Application.Workbooks.Open("D:\F1.xls")

wb.ActiveSheet.Cells(1, 1) = "22"
wb.Save
wb.Close

End Sub
```

14.4 Protect a workbook

We can use below macro code to protect workbook.

```
ActiveWorkbook.protect Structure:=True,
Windows:=False
```

15. Automating Worksheets using Macros

In this chapter you will learn about automating the worksheet tasks using macros like....

1. Inserting a new worksheet
2. Hiding a worksheet
3. Unhiding a worksheet
4. Deleteing existing worksheet
5. Protecting worksheet
6. Rearranging the worksheets
7. Changing the colour of the worksheet tab
8. Copy worksheet from one workbook to another
9. Moving worksheet across workbooks.

15.1 Inserting new worksheet

Below Example Shows how we can create a new Worksheet using Macro.

In below code, we are trying to add new worksheet with name –"sagar" in current workbook. If the worksheet with name – "sagar" already exists, macro code will show pop up message saying the sheet already exists. If the sheet does not exist, new sheet will be added.

```
mySheet = "Sagar"
On Error Resume Next

Temp = Worksheets(mySheet).Name

If Err.Number = 0 Then
```

```
    MsgBox "The sheet already Exists "


Else

    Err.Clear
    Worksheets.Add.Name = mySheet
    MsgBox "The New sheet Created "

End if
```

This is how we can create a new worksheet using a VBA macro in Excel 2010/2003/2007.

15.2 Hide a worksheet

Below Example will hide a worksheet3.

```
Sheet3.Visible = False
```

15.3 Unhide a worksheet

Below Example will unhide a worksheet3.

```
Sheet3.Visible = True
```

15.4 Sort the worksheets in worksbook

Below Example will sort the worksheets in alphbetical order and then move them accordingly.

```
  Mysheets= Sheets.Count

    For i = 1 To Mysheets- 1

        For j = i + 1 To Mysheets

If Sheets(j).Name < Sheets(i).Name Then
   Sheets(j).Move before:=Sheets(i)
   ' Swap the sheets
End If

        Next j

    Next i
```

Above code will sort the worksheets in Workbook using Excel Macro in 2007/2010/2003.

15.5 Move worksheets

Below macro code will move worksheet sagar from current workbook to another open workbook – Book1.xlsm

The last statement will determine the position where you have added a worksheet. In below code we have added the worksheet after sheet1.

Sheets("sagar").Select

```
Sheets("sagar").move
After:=Workbooks("Book1.xlsm").Sheets(1)
```

To move the sheet to same workbook, you will have below syntax.

```
Sheets("sagar").move After:=Sheets(1)
```

15.6 Copy worksheets

Below macro code will copy worksheet sheet4 from current workbook to another open workbook – Book1.xlsm

The last statement will determine the position where you have added a worksheet. In below code we have added the worksheet after sheet at index 1.

```
Sheets("Sheet4").Select

Sheets("Sheet4").Copy
Before:=Workbooks("Book1.xlsm").Sheets(1)
```

To copy the sheet to same workbook, you will have below syntax.

```
Sheets("Sheet4").Copy Before:=Sheets(1)
```

15.7 Delete worksheet from a workbook

Below macro code will delete the worksheet with name sheet1 from current workbook.

```
Application.DisplayAlerts = False

Sheets("Sheet1").Delete
```

Please note that we have set the DisplayAlerts property to false to suppres the dialog window. Otherwise You will encouter below warning message saying – data may exist in the sheet(s) selected for deletion. To permanently delete the data, Press Delete.

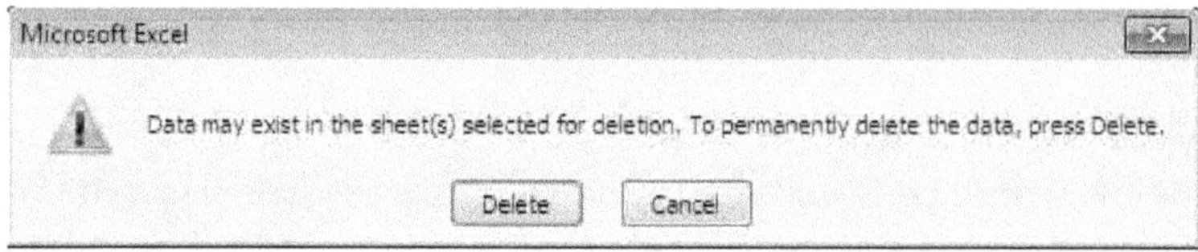

15.8 How to rename worksheet

If you want to change the name of existing worksheet, it is very simple to do in macro. Below code will rename the sheet3 to Sales.

```
Sheets("Sheet3").Select

Sheets("Sheet3").Name = "sales"
```

15.9 How to Change Tab color of worksheet

Below macro code will change the tab color of the sheet3.

```
Sheets("sales").Select

With ActiveWorkbook.Sheets("sales").Tab

.ThemeColor = xlThemeColorLight2

.TintAndShade = -0.249977111117893

End With
```

16. Manipulating data using Excel Macro

In this chapter you will learn about how you can process or analyse the data in the cell or range of cells using macros like....

1. Sorting data in a column
2. Filtering the data in a column
3. Protecting cells
4. Inserting and deleting the rows
5. Inserting and deleting the columns
6. Formatting the cells
7. Finding the blanks cells, rows and columns
8. Adding functions in the cells
9. Trim the cell values
10. Replacing the cell values
11. Copying rows, columns or range
12. Cutting the rows, columns or range

16.1 Inserting and deleting the rows

1) Insert rows and columns

Example - Below code will add a new column at B. Old data at column B will be shifted to right.

```
activeworksheet.Columns("B:B).Select
Selection.Insert
```

This is how we can add column at any position in excel using macro.

Example - Below code will add/ Insert blank row in Excel Sheet

Macro Code / Syntax to Add new Row in Excel.

```
Rows("6:6").Select
 Selection.Insert Shift:=xlDown,
CopyOrigin:=xlFormatFromLeftOrAbove
```

Above code will add / Insert new row at row number 6. Old row at row number 6 will be pushed down.

This is how we can add or insert new / Blank row in excel.

2)Delete existing rows and columns

```
activeworksheet.Columns("B:B").Select
Selection.Delete

activeworksheet.Rows("1:1").Select
Selection.Delete
```

3) Find blank rows and cells

Below Example will count all blank cells from given range in the worksheets

VBA Macro Code / Syntax :

```
n =
Range("h3:h30").Cells.SpecialCells(xlCe
llTypeBlanks).Count
MsgBox n        'Print all blank cells

Here xlCellTypeBlanks means that cell is
blank.


n =
Range("h3:h30").Cells.SpecialCells(xlCellTy
peConstants).Count
MsgBox n     ' Print all cells with constant
values not formulas
```

This is how we can find out the blank cells in Excel Macro.

4) Select Entire Row/Column in Excel VBA Macro

Example - We can select entire row or column vey easily using below code.

Code and Syntax :

To Select Entire Row No 2 –

```
Workbooks("Book1").Sheets("Sheet1").Ran
ge("2:2").Font.Bold = True
```

To Select Entire Column A –

```
Workbooks("Book1").Sheets("Sheet1").Ran
ge("A:A").Font.Bold = True
```

To Select Cell A1 -

```
Workbooks("Book1").Sheets("Sheet1").Range("
A1").Font.Bold = True
```

To Select Cell Range –

```
Workbooks("Book1").Sheets("Sheet1").Ran
ge("A1:B8").Font.Bold = True
```

To Select Multiple Cell Range –

```
Workbooks("Book1").Sheets("Sheet1").Ran
ge("A1:B8,G3:I9").Font.Bold = True
```

To Select Multiple Columns sequentially –

```
Workbooks("Book1").Sheets("Sheet1").Ran
ge("A:C").Font.Bold = True
```

To Select Multiple Columns Not sequentially –

```
Workbooks("Book1").Sheets("Sheet1").Ran
ge("A:A,C:C").Font.Bold = True
'Here Columns A and C will be selected.
```

5) Different Excel Cell Types in VBA Macros

Below is the list of All Cell Types in VBA Macros

xlCellTypeAllFormatConditions - Cells of any format
xlCellTypeAllValidation - validation criteria Cells
xlCellTypeBlanks - Empty /Blank cells
xlCellTypeComments - Cells with comments
xlCellTypeConstants - Cells with constants values
xlCellTypeFormulas - Cells having formulas
xlCellTypeLastCell - last cell in the used range
xlCellTypeSameFormatConditions - Cells having the same format
xlCellTypeSameValidation - Cells having the same validation criteria
xlCellTypeVisible - All visible cells

Example -

```
msgbox
Range("h3:h30").Cells.SpecialCells(xlCe
llTypeBlanks).Count
```

This will print the number of cells in given range that are of type - xlCellTypeBlanks. Means it will print the count of blank cells.

6) Clear contents of certain cells in Excel sheet

Example -

In below example I am going to show you how we can clear the contents of specified cells in excel sheet.
I will also show you how we can use macro to clear the contents of entire row or column.

Code and Syntax to clear the contents of specified cells using macro.

Code to clear the contents of certain cell.

```
Range("A18").Select
Selection.ClearContents
```

Code to clear the contents of multiple cells.

```
Range("A2:B22").Select
  ' clear contents of a range
Selection.ClearContents
```

Code to clear the contents of Entire row in Excelsheet

```
rows("2:2").Select
Selection.ClearContents
```

Code to clear the contents of Entire Column in Excelsheet

```
columns("A:A").Select
Selection.ClearContents
```

In similar way we can clear the contents of any cells, ranges in excel sheet using VBA macro. It is just two step process.

- Select the area/region you want to clear.
- Use Selection.ClearContents statement.

16.2 Formatting the cells

1) Change the font color and size of Cell in Excel

Below example will change the font size as well as font color of text inside the cell in worksheet in Excel Workbook.

Code and Syntax

```
 Activeworksheet.Range("A1").select

    Selection.Font.Italic = True
'make the font italic in macro

    Selection.Font.Bold = False
'make the font bold in macro
```

```
    Selection.Font.Underline =
xlUnderlineStyleSingle
'Underline the macro

    Selection.Font.ThemeColor =
xlThemeColorLight2
' Change the color of cell

    Selection.Font.TintAndShade =
0.399975585192419
'Change the shade of color

    Selection.Font.Name = "Calibri"
'Change the name of font

    Selection.Font.Size = 20
'Change the size of macro

    Selection.Font.Strikethrough =
False                       'Other
features of font like strikethrough

    Selection.Font.Superscript = False
'Subscript, Shadow, Underline etc.

    Selection.Font.Subscript = False

    Selection.Font.OutlineFont = False

     Selection.Font.Shadow = False

     Selection.Font.Underline =
xlUnderlineStyleSingle

  Selection.Font.Color = -16776961

  Selection.Font.TintAndShade = 0
```

2) Set the background color of cell using Excel VBA Macro

In below example, I have changed the background color of the A1 using a Macro.

Code / Syntax : -

```
Range("A1").Interior.ColorIndex = 8
 'Change the background color of Cell
A1

Range("A1".EntireRow.Interior.ColorInde
x = 8
 'Change the background color of Entire
Row.
```

This is how we can change the background color of Cell/Range in Excel using VBA Macro

3) Changing data in cells relative to each other

We can enter data in the relative cells using offset property. In below example we have set the value 22 and set the font color of the cell to green which is placed at

2 rows down and 3 columns to the right of cell A1

```
Sub offset_property()

'Offset property is used to access the cell
in a relative manner

Worksheets(1).Cells(1, 1).Offset(2,
3).value = 22

Worksheets(1).Cells(1, 1).Offset(2,
3).Font.Color = vbGreen


End Sub
```

4) Change the font of multiple rows in excel macro

Below macro code illustrates how we can change the font of multiple rows.

```
Sub change_font_multiple_rows()

'We can select multiple rows using below
syntax

'For single row
'In below example we have changed the font
of the row number 1
Worksheets(1).Range("1:1").Font.Bold =
False


'For multiple sequential rows
'In below example we have changed the font
of all the rows from 1 to 4
```

```
Worksheets(1).Range("1:4").Font.Bold =
False

'For multiple non-sequential rows
Worksheets(1).Range("1:1,3:3").Font.Bold =
False

'Please note that you can not only change
the font of the rows but also change the
other properties like alignment, font
style, indentation, border of the cells,
color etc

'Alternative way to select the row
Worksheets(1).Rows(1).Font.Bold = False

'In below example we have change the color
of the border of rows 1,2 and 4 to red
Set row124 = Union(Rows(1), Rows(2),
Rows(4))
row124.Borders.LineStyle = xlNone
row124.Borders.Color = vbRed

End Sub
```

5) Convert the data type of cell value

We can convert the given variable in any desired format. For example we we have a string as 09-jan-2013, we can convert it into date as mentioned below.

```
Sub conversion()

  date1 = CDate("09-jan-2013")
  MsgBox"Data type of date1 is"&
TypeName(date1)

```

```
'If the input to cdate function is not a
valid date, type mismatch error will occur
'Similarly you can convert the string into
integer, float ect

  MsgBox CInt("243.6 ")

'To convert the number into string, you can
use cstr function

  no = 2344
  MsgBox CStr(no)

End Sub
```

6) Extract the part of cell value or string

you can use below functions to extract the part of the string

```
Sub extractString()

MsgBox Left("Lalu Prasad", 4)
 'get 4 characters from left side of
string
 'output - Lalu
 'Left function will get the specified
number of characters from left side of
the string

MsgBox Right("Lalu Prasad", 6)
 'get 6 characters from the right side
of the string
 'Right function will get the specified
number of characters from right side of
the string
 'Output - Prasad
```

```
MsgBox Mid("Lalu Prasad", 6, 6)
 'get 6 characters starting from index
6
 'Mid function is used to get the fixed
length portion of string starting from
given position or index
 'Output - Prasad

End Sub
```

7) Excel Macro to add leading zero to cell value

Excel Macro to add leading zero to any cell.

```
Sub addLeadingZero()

   'get the value from cell
   x = Sheet1.Cells(1, 1)
    'add leading zero

   x = "'000" & x

    'print value with zero
   MsgBox x

    'store value back in cell
   Sheet1.Cells(1, 1) = x

End Sub
```

16.3 Worksheet and Workbook

1) Select multiple ranges in a worksheet in excel macro

Below macro code shows how we can select multiple range like `A1:B8,C1:D8`

```
Sub select_multiple_range()

'We can select multiple range using below
code

Worksheets(1).Range("A1:B8,C1:D8").Font.Bol
d = True


'In above code we have selected 2 ranges.
First one is A1:B8 and other is from C1:D8

'To access each range separately, we can
use below syntax

'In below code we have displayed the total
number of cells in first range (area)

MsgBox
Worksheets(1).Range("A1:B8,C1:D8").Areas(1)
.Cells.Count

End Sub
```

2) Clear the contents of entire worksheet in excel macro

```
Sub clear_worksheet_contents()

'We can select all cells from the given
sheet by using below code

Worksheets(1).Cells.Clear

'Above code will delete the data as well as
formatting from all cells from the sheet1

End Sub
```

3) Access the worksheets by its index in excel macro

We can refer to the worksheets by it's index using below syntax. In below example we have used the sheet at index 1. Index of the leftmost worksheet is always 1 and it is incremented by 1 from left to right. We we move or add new worksheets in a workbook, the indices of the existing sheets also change.

```
Sub access_worksheets_by_index()

Worksheets(1).Select

End Sub
```

4) Access the worksheets by its name in excel macro

Below procedure will access the worksheets by its names. We can access the worksheets by its name by below syntax. In below example we have selected the sheet with the name balancesheet.

```
Sub access_worksheets_by_name()

Worksheets("balancesheet").Select

End Sub
```

This is how we can access the sheets using sheet name.

5) Delete multiple work sheets with excel macro

Below sub procedure will delete 2 sheets with name sheet2 and sheet3. We can select multiple worksheets by using below syntax.

```
Sub access_worksheets_by_name()

Worksheets("balancesheet").Select

'This is how we can access the sheets using
sheet name

End Sub
```

6) Add new workbook using excel macro

Below code will add new workbook and write some data into it and save it as well.

```
Sub Add_New_Workbook()
```

```
'We can add new workbook by using add
method of workbooks collection

Set new_workbook = Workbooks.Add

'access the cells in first sheet from the
newly added workbook
new_workbook.Worksheets(1).Cells(1, 1) =
"obama"

'save new workbook to hard disk
new_workbook.SaveAs "c:\temp.xlsx"

'close new workbook
new_workbook.Close

'release the memory of the object
associated with new_workbook
Set new_workbook = Nothing

End Sub
```

7) How to find out if particular Worksheet Exists Using Excel VBA Macro

Below Code/Example can be used to find if given worksheet exists in Workbook or not.

Macro Code to check if particular Worksheet Exists or Not in Workbook.

```
 Dim mySheet
    mySheet = "Sagar"
    On Error Resume Next
```

```
    temp = Worksheets(mySheet ).Name
    If Err.Number = 0 Then
        MsgBox "Given Sheet Exists "
    Else
        Err.Clear
     MsgBox "Given Sheet Does not Exist"

End If
```

8) Access Sheets (Worksheets, Charts, Dialogs) Using Name/Index in Excel Macro

Below Example will show you how we can Access various sheets like worksheets, charts, modules, and dialog sheets using name in Macro.

Macro Code / Syntax -

```
Worksheets("Sheet1").Activate
Charts("Chart1").Activate
DialogSheets("Dialog1").Activate
```

In above code we are accessing the sheet1, chart1 and dialog1 using Excel Macro.

16.4 Files

1) Read data from text file

Excel macro to read a text file

```
Sub readFile()

Dim myfso As Scripting.FileSystemObject
Dim stream As Scripting.TextStream

Set myfso=New Scripting.FileSystemObject

'open text file in read mode.
Set stream=myfso.OpenTextFile ("c:\F1.txt",
ForReading,True)

MsgBox stream.ReadAll

End Sub
```

2) Create text file

Please note that to perform file related functions in your project, you will have to add reference of microsoft script runtime. Here is the excel macro code to create a text file.

```
Sub createFile()

Dim myfso As Scripting.FileSystemObject

Dim stream As Scripting.TextStream

Set myfso=New Scripting.FileSystemObject

Set stream =
myfso.CreateTextFile("c:\F1.txt", True)

'Create text file at given path

stream.Write ("This is file creation demo.
if file exists, it will be overwritten")

'Write data into opened file's stream
```

```
stream.Close

Set stream = Nothing

Set myfso = Nothing

End Sub
```

This is how You can create a file in excel macro.

3) Create and use dictionary object in excel macro

Please note that to use dictionary in your project, you will have to add reference of microsoft script runtime. Dictionary object allows you to store the elements in dynamic way using keys. Unlike arrays where values are stored using index, dictionary uses keys to store values.

```
Sub createDictionary()

Dim d1 As Scripting.Dictionary

'To add key in dictionary,use below code
Set d1 = New Scripting.Dictionary
d1.Add "sachin", 41
d1.Add "dhoni", 32

'To get the value at particular key
MsgBox d1.Item("sachin")

'to remove key from dictionary
d1.Remove "dhoni"

'To get all keys from the dictionary, use
below code
keyArray = d1.Keys
```

```
'to check if given key exists in the
dictionary

If d1.Exists("sachin") Then
    MsgBox "Key sachin exists"
Else
    MsgBox "Key sachin does not exist"
End If

'To remove all keys from dictionary, use
below code

d1.RemoveAll

End Sub
```

This is how you can use dictionary object in excel macro You can store the values from 2 columns as key value pair in dictionary.

16.5 Array in excel

1) Create and use array in excel macro

Arrays are used to store large number of elements in sequence. There are 2 types of Arrays in Excel Macro.

1.Fixed Size Array
2.Dynamic Array

```
Sub createArray()

Dim a(11)
a(0) = "sagar"
a(1) = 2
MsgBox a(1) & a(0)

'Or you can also create array like this
a=Array("sagar","amol","sachin",33,44, 55)
'*******Dynamic Array********
Dim b()

ReDim Preserve b(3)

'Above statement will resize the array to
size 4
'Preserve statement will keep the existing
values in the array intact

ReDim Preserve b(6)

'Again resize array to size of 7

End Sub
```

This is how we can array to store any number of values.

2) Filter Array

```
Sub Macro1()

    arr = Array("January", "February",
"March", "April", "May", "June", "July",
```

```
"August", "September", "October",
"November", "December")

    filt = Filter(arr, "J")

    For Each x In filt
        MsgBox (x)
    Next

End Sub
```

Output :- January
June
July

3) Join Array

```
Sub Macro1()

    arr = Array("Sunday","Monday",
"Tuesday","Wednesday","Thusday",
"Friday","Saturday")

    MsgBox (Join(arr))

End Sub
```

Output:- Sunday Monday Tuesday Wednesday Thusday Friday Saturday

4) Ubound

```
Sub Macro1()

    arr = Array("Jan", "Feb", "Mar", "Apr",
"May", "Jun", "Jul", "Aug", "Sep")
```

```
    MsgBox (LBound(arr))

    'Print Array Length
    MsgBox (UBound(arr))

End Sub
```

Output: 0
8

16.6 Create modules in Excel Macro

Modules are used to store the related procedures and functions

1.Modules contain the functions that provide unique functionality
2.We can group similar functions and procedures in separate module
3.Class module contains properties and methods of that particular class
4.For example - we can create a student class which can be used to store/retrieve student properties like student name, student id, student address etc.

16.7 How to pause the execution of Macro in Excel

In below example, you will see how we can pause the execution of macro before executing next statement. Please note that wscript is not available in Excel VBA Macro. It is available only in vbscript.

Code and Syntax for making the programm wait in Excel VBA is given below.

```
a = 10

Application.Wait(Now()+TimeValue("0
:00:11"))

msgbox a
```

As you can see in above code, I have used Application.Wait statement.
if you execute this code, you will see that value in a is prompted after 11 seconds.

To wait for say 10 mins, you will have to use below code

```
a = 10

Application.Wait(Now()+TimeValue("0:10:
00"))

msgbox a
```

So here the format of TimeValue is -

TimeValue("hh:mm:ss")) - So you can give any value in hour/minute/second to make macro wait for that particular time.

16.8 Get the month name of given date

```
Sub getMonthName()

  'Print current month name

  MsgBox MonthName(Month(Now))

  'To print month name of any given
date you can use below macro code

  MsgBox MonthName(Month("09-jan-
1988"))

End Sub
```

16.9 Get the stock data from yahoo finance

Below procedure can be used to get the stock information from yahoo finance.

```
Sub getYahooFinance()

'Below script will download the quotes
for given symbol from yahoo finance
'more info at ->
http://www.jarloo.com/yahoo_finance/

'qURL =
"http://finance.yahoo.com/d/quotes.csv?
s=AAPL+GOOG+MSFT&f=nv"
'http://finance.yahoo.com/d/quotes.csv?
s=AAPL+GOOG+MSFT&f=nv

qURL =
"http://ichart.finance.yahoo.com/table.
csv?s=rcom.BO&ignore=.csv"
```

```
With
Sheet1.QueryTables.Add(Connection:="URL
;"&qURL,
Destination:=Sheet1.Range("A1"))

       .BackgroundQuery = True
       .TablesOnlyFromHTML = False
       .Refresh BackgroundQuery:=False
       .SaveData = True
End With

End Sub
```

16.10 Get stock finance data from Google NSE BSE

Below program will get stock/finance information in xml format from google finance.
You can give the stocks from NSE and BSE as well.

```
'Specify the url to connect to
URL="http://www.google.com/ig/api?stock
=rcom"
Set objHTTP=CreateObject
("MSXML2.XMLHTTP")

Call objHTTP.Open("GET", URL, False)
objHTTP.Send

'The response comes in the form of xml
stream.

MsgBox (objHTTP.ResponseText)
```

16.11 Excel Macro to process xml file

```
Sub processXML()

Set xDoc =
CreateObject("MSXML2.DOMDocument")

'to load the xml string
'xDoc.LoadXML
("<book><str>hello</str></book>")
'to load xml from file, use below
syntax

xDoc.Load ("c:\abc.xml")
'Display all elements and their values
Call DisplayNode(xDoc.ChildNodes, 0)

MsgBox str1

'We can also use xpath to get the
collection of nodes
xDoc.setProperty "SelectionLanguage",
"XPath"

strPath = "//book"

Set nodelist =
xDoc.DocumentElement.SelectNodes(strPat
h)

MsgBox "No of Nodes Found by using
xpath is -> " & nodelist.Length & "
Node"
```

```
Set xDoc = Nothing

End Sub
```

Recursive function to traverse all the nodes inside xml file/ String

```
Public Sub DisplayNode(ByRef Nodes,
ByVal Indent)

   Dim xNode
   Indent = Indent + 2

For Each xNode In Nodes

 If xNode.NodeType = NODE_TEXT Then

    str1 = str1 & " " &
xNode.ParentNode.nodeName & ":" &
xNode.NodeValue

End If

 If xNode.HasChildNodes Then

    DisplayNode xNode.ChildNodes,
Indent

 End If

Next
```

```
End Sub
```

16.12 Display a dialog box

We can display message box / dialog box with yes/no buttons in excel macro using msgbox function

```
Sub messageBox()

ret = MsgBox("Yes - No Buttons",
vbYesNoCancel, "MessageBox Macro")
'Please note that second parameter in
the function msgbox decided which
buttons to display on the dialog 'box.

If ret = 6 Then
   MsgBox "You cliked on Yes"
ElseIf ret = 7 Then
   MsgBox "You cliked on No"
Else
  'ret = 2
  MsgBox "You cliked on Cancel"
End If

End Sub
```

16.13 Macro to calculate system idle time in Excel.

In below example, I have shown how we can find the system idle time using excel vba macro.

Code and Syntax to calculate system idle time.
In below code, GetIdleTime() function returns the number of seconds the system has been idle for.
Here idle means that there is no input from user from keyboard or mouse.

```
Private Type LASTINPUTINFO
  cbSize As Long
  dwTime As Long
End Type

'*****************************

Private Declare Sub GetLastInputInfo
Lib "user32" (ByRef plii As
LASTINPUTINFO)
Private Declare Function GetTickCount
Lib "kernel32" () As Long

'******************************

Function GetIdleTime() As Single
  Dim a As LASTINPUTINFO
  a.cbSize = LenB(a)
  GetLastInputInfo a
  GetIdleTime= (GetTickCount -
a.dwTime) / 1000
End Function

'********************************
```

```
Sub check()
        Application.Wait (Now() +
TimeValue("0:00:11"))
   ' make the system idle for 11 sec.
Donot type from keyboard or click from
mouse
        MsgBox getIdleTime()
End Sub
```

LASTINPUTINFO is a structure defined by microsoft and it Contains the time of the last input.

GetTickCount functions gets the number of milliseconds that have elapsed since the system was started, up to 49.7 days.

When you will execute above programm, you will be prompted approx. 11 as system idle time